The Inconvenience of Grief

Lannie Stabile

Advance Praise for *The Inconvenience of Grief*

"Lannie Stabile's *The Inconvenience of Grief* is the old, locked trunk hidden in your parents' closet, the one that holds every secret, every memory and keepsake. And moving through this collection, we are privy to the experience of rummaging through it all. Stabile's speaker plucks each memory from the pile, examines them with the emotional dexterity of the adult daughter who finally understands how her childhood trauma has shaped her. Witnessing this emotional archiving is to witness how we reclaim power over our histories—on the other side of understanding it is the power to remember it, to forget it, to forgive those who authored it."
—Dr Taylor Byas, author, instructor, freelance editor

"Lannie Stabile's *The Inconvenience of Grief* is one of those books I could describe as the point of contact between the waters of Styx and Charon's boat—a place where raw grief bumps against the quotidian. Or I could say it possesses that rare honesty and dark humor known only by those who've lost a parent. I could say it's a book steeped in a simple truth: the inconvenience of grief is that we are alive to feel it. I could say this, and so much more, because Stabile has written one of those perfect books that is huge and all-encompassing, a book in possession of a thousand horizons. But the biggest endorsement I can give is also my bluntest: I wish, in the years after my mother died, I'd owned this book. Stabile's *The Inconvenience of Grief* is the kind of poetry you'll think about before you fall asleep, or on the long silences driving to a family barbecue, or in those moments when a winter wind braids through your laughter. Buy this book, read it, and you'll find yourself returning to it over and over for the rest of your life."
—Todd Dillard, author of *Ways We Vanish*

"'We have mourned enough, gone visiting too many traveling carnivals', Lannie Stabile writes in her newest collection *The Inconvenience of Grief*. And her poems hit hard, beat after beat in that search for closure. Stabile approaches loss in the most honest, unadorned way—and yet somehow never sinks, even in the deepest, most vulnerable waters. She invites us to take a deep breath and dive in, too, and I'm so glad I did. What a marvel this collection is!"

—Hannah Grieco, editor of *Already Gone*
and *And If That Mockingbird Don't Sing*

Copyright © 2023 Lannie Stabile

All Rights Reserved. This book or any portion thereof may not be reproduced, in whole or in part, in any form (beyond that permitted by Sections 107 and 108 of the U.S Copyright Law and except by reviewers for the public press), without the express written permission of the publisher except for the use of brief quotations in a book review.

Stabile, Lannie author

The Inconvenience of Grief / Lannie Stabile

Poems

ISBN: 979-8-9869524-2-0

Library of Congress Control Number: 2023942377

Edited by: Beth Gordon
Book Design: Amanda McLeod
Cover Art:. Sami Aksu via Pexels & MarjanNo via Pixabay.
Cover Design: Amanda McLeod

PUBLISHER
Animal Heart Press
Thetford Center, Vermont 05075
www.animalheartpress.net

The Inconvenience of Grief

Lannie Stabile

*To my brother, Eric.
Thanks for coming back to me.*

*And to our mother.
You'd be proud of how we've grieved.*

Table of Contents

If You Want to Be a Good Day	15
A Standing Dinner Invitation to My Anger	16
A Parable of Wanderlust	18
The Time My Brother Doused Himself in Gasoline...	19
The Grand Canyon Is My Father	20
The Wall	21
My Birth Has Often Been About Secrets	22
My Brother Was a Bomb	24
In Tandem	25
My Greatest Fear Is Turning into My Mother	26
Time Stands Still at My Local Kroger	27
Hard Things	28
The Second Is Fear	30
Papa Bear	31
An Influencer Follows Me on Twitter, and It Feels Like...	32
February 17, 2021	33
Sibling Rivalry	34
When My Father Died	35
I Killed My Mother	36
The First Year Without Her	37
Fatality	38
It's the Year 2000, Cosmic Bowling Has Started, and I Think...	39
Dear Photo of My Dead Mother, Circa 1978	40
Whiskers	42
Oophagy (or Intrauterine Cannibalism)	43

My Mother Deftly Misses the Point	44
If Found	45
Meet Me at the Funeral Home, I'll Be the One Cussing…	46
Death	47
The First Christmas Without Her	48
Words Between the Daughter and the Mother	49
Self Portrait with Cremains	50
Rite of Passage	51
"I Love You Like Baby Hitler Loved His Easy Bake Oven"	52
The First Thanksgiving Without Her	53
A Devotion, of Sorts	54
Pantoum for Mom and Punxsutawney Phil	55
You Ask Me How I Am but Never Wait for the Answer	56
The Onion Never Grieves for the Tears It Causes	57
She Is Unavailable for Lunch	58
The First Halloween Without Her	59
Explaining My Introversion to a Genocidist Sympathizer	60
The Most Dangerous Fish	61
A Single Stitch	62
Suicide Attempt, #Unknown	63
Piece by Piece in Lakeland	64
The Child Was Not Invited to the Funeral	65
The First Fourth of July Without Her	66
The Feedback in a Conch Shell Is Both the Ocean and…	67
Red Skies at Morn	69
The Day My Mother Is Intubated, I Find a Pimple on My Chin	70
brother, brother, brother	71

To the Lonely Spark	72
A Widow Offering	75
The First Birthday Without Her	76
And I Will Carry This Burden	77
Ode to 1997	79
Karen Kilgariff Says the Death of a Mother Is Like...	80
Where to Start	81
Happy Mask Shop	82
My Father Wears a Hawaiian Shirt to Die In	83
The First Easter Without Her	84
I Tell Myself She Ran Away	85
I Won't Be Able to Make It to the Cemetery Today...	87
I Just Emailed an Estate Lawyer Regarding My Mother's Will...	88
On Pennsylvania Road	89
Pot Roast, Unburnt	90
My Worship	91
The First Month Without Her	92
The Only Thing I Wanted Was for You to Live	93
The Birch Is Too Proud	94
I Imagine My Mother Apologizing	95
My Brother Puts Me in a Boston Crab Underwater, and I...	96
Rough Draft	97
After Further Consideration, She Has His Ears	98
Birding	99
Death Leaves Something Behind	100
Now. Then. Always.	101
Cremation: Mother	102

Arguing the Etymology of "OK" with Someone Who's Always…	103
The First Day Without Her	104
Acknowledgements	107
Author's Notes	110
About the Author	111

If You Want to Be a Good Day

If you want to be a good day, be Christmas two years ago. An unseasonable 50 degrees. Not a wink of snow in sight. Big family stuffed into too small living room. Eight folding chairs around a six-foot card table. Bird picked over. Potatoes flaking. Gravy graying in the old Country Crock container. A contractor bag of discarded wrapping paper bulging by the front door, Mom's oxygen tank alive and hissing in the corner. But wait. Watch as Mom unrolls her trove of one- and two-dollar lottery tickets with an eyebrow wiggle. *You gotta play to win,* she tempts, pulling Monopoly: Go from a Walmart shopping bag. An hour, several scratching pennies, and a $10 dollar winner later, the pumpkin pie is done. The blue can of Reddi-wip passes from hand to hand.

A Standing Dinner Invitation to My Anger

I wish you'd come 'round for dinner.
When you're not here
the plates just sit flat and unresponsive,
staring at me like disembodied heads
with tight secrets crushed between their ceramic lips.
The chairs don't wobble or tip or upend themselves.
They pretend four legs can't dance better than two.
We, of course, know better.
And I can still hear our music if I strain hard enough.
Conversation drips slow and painful,
a flawed faucet leading gradually to madness.
I sip and I sip and I sip and I sip and I sip and …

I carved the roast last night.
As steel slid through the tender breast of the beast,
I imagined your hands as my hands
and its flesh as their flesh.
You always knew what to do with sharp objects.

Though I've been screaming since I got here,
every highball glass remains unshattered.
I'm in a state of suppression
sealed within the politeness of sugar bowls
served in neat, winsome cubes, one or two at a time.
Poison dissolving into complicit puddles.

Do you know the torture of sitting silent?
Sycophantic tongues are careless and efficient.
Guests tasting the soft joy in the room,
licking the charm from the walls,
lapping up any loveliness we have managed to hoard.
I want to rip the ribbons from their throats,
and hang them with the pretty bows.

But you're not here.

So I fold these dainty, untainted hands in my lap,
regardless of how blood-thirsty they may be.
I cross my ankles like kindling.
I sit tall; I sit straight and wretched.
Of course, I choke on the courses.
Compromise doesn't slide down easily.
But the guests run their fingers along my dissent,
coaxing the chicken bone into place,
and they call it love.
I don't know how much longer I can hold my breath.

I wish you'd come 'round for dinner.

I'll set a place for you.

A Parable of Wanderlust
A double acrostic

Please know it wasn't about you. Roads have always crooked fingers. Tell Dad rent was paid; coin was siphoned from the bitterness you gave me. The pea on my mattress digs into the women I ladder into bed each night. I know you didn't intend for the town to sink its teeth in me. Stars straighten up, unjamming. I thought we could finally try this fault-line family. We have mourned enough, gone visiting too many traveling carnivals. I want to come home, but the tent alone has turned cold. Its welcoming skeleton crew. Here is my handful of lonely dirt. May it bring you more solid ground than you received from your daughter.

The Time My Brother Doused Himself in Gasoline and Struck a Match Has Stolen the Remote

We don't talk about it:

the smell of sulfur in the living room,

gas can lurking near the beat up recliner
he and I fought over every Saturday morning,

the gentle *drip* of accelerant from his shirt tail
onto the neglected hardwood, original from 1924,

singed skin lingering in the siren air,

how the match fell from his fingers
and we all held our breath.

The Grand Canyon Is My Father
A golden shovel

He was the kind of boulder it
                        takes
                                a millennium of river to kill. His titanic guts
butted up against the to-
                    pography of siblings, and he would be
                            a pebble if they asked. Or an

                obelus organ-
                        izing two legacies of a donor.

The Wall

Mother. Ravaged. By. Soft. Heart. By. Men. With. Dead. Nails. Gums. Livers. Fists. Daughter. Witnessed. Weeping. Bruising. Cowering. Fridge. Bears. Broom. Smile. He. Tried. To. Beat. Her. Clean. Steered. Us. Into. Oncoming. Traffic. Shook. Hands. With. Kitten. Neck. Called. Me. Cunt. Asked. Me. To. Piss. For. Him. Camel. Cigarettes. Mohawk. Vodka. Scents. That. Peel. Skin. From. My. Bones. Pungent. Dependence. Sweat. Soaked. Sheets. Why. She. Let. Him. Stay. Hoped. Big. Brother. Would. Defend. Instead. He. Picked. Up. Tricks. Picked. At. Crusted. Family. Scabs. Picked. On. Those. Who. Held. Him. New. Phallic. Fear. Always. Afraid. To. Tell. Him. No. Always. Terrified. He. Would. Ignite. Family. Does. Not. Betray. Family. Mother. Said. When. I. Dialed. When. Hounds. Fed. She. Had. Excuses. I. Have. Scars. Steel. Against. My. Back. His. Minted. Grip. On. My. Arms. He. Forced. Her. To. Arthritic. Knees. The. Closest. I've. Been. To. Insanity. I. Cut. Him. With. Knuckles. Teeth. Lodged. Inside. Calf. Jaundiced. Oozing. She. Let. Me. Leave. I. Haven't. Killed. A. Man. Yet. But. I. Have. Loved. One. I. Have. Made. My. Mother's. Excuses. Such. Softness. Such. Compassionate. Blood.

My Birth Has Often Been About Secrets

My mother fell off a concrete porch and woke
in the summer spireas with knowledge of my
blooming body.

> The radiologist ran her gloved finger
> over the Rorschach flower, pointing
> out male privilege and a healthy
> heartbeat. My father cried when I
> was born inverted. But I was still
> named for him.

The year I was gifted both a swing set and a
party, I was also banned from competing. *The
games and prizes are for the guests*, mother
said, plucking my petals. But I swung the
highest and leapt the farthest anyway.

> Ronald Reagan died the week I
> turned 17. The very day my friends
> gathered beneath lush canopies in
> the park to celebrate. I could think
> only of the dead president and how
> he ruined my hot dog.

I knew a man who threw a party once he
fucked 100 women. He called it an induction
to the Century Club. The night after my best
friend slept with him, I spent my birthday
chewing the perfect medium ribeye her
boyfriend grilled for me, wilting with every
bite.

> A pregnant sister revealed her quiet
> thorn to me on Mother's Day. Two
> weeks later, the news rattled in my

>   own unsettled belly, as I cut the cake
>   into controlled triangles. The word
>   *mum* thumping behind my lips.

My mother called yesterday. She sang to me
and asked about my life. I was sitting on the
patio, sweeping away the helicopter seeds,
thinking *for once, she's asking about me.*

My Brother Was a Bomb

I surveil his ignition hands
puckered by bloodline, touch

the memories steep with pain:
when he dunked my head
between swamp jaws,
tucked me into
a Boston Crab in the hotel pool,
drowned himself
in gasoline and struck

a match. And I try to picture
that grinning summer
we jumped
like mullet in and out

of hose-filled barrels,
the hot pavement hissing
as water slapped

in escape. I swam then
with a time bomb and
called him *bubby*
because I couldn't pronounce

brother.

In Tandem
A golden shovel

He should have been one more stick in the spoke. Why
couldn't he have wobbled like all muddy tires? Why couldn't
he have been a man that said, *Look Ma, no hands!* as the
road rolled out uneven? Another asshole who rode her bicycle
like the wind, then was gone with it. No kickstand
on the hot summer pavement. Instead, one by
one, my father peddled faith into us. The church, itself,
quietly consisting of our small, tandem family. It
was the last time wind was ever at my back. When I was
balloon and vesper. It takes so much energy to mourn for two.

And I am so tired.

My Greatest Fear Is Turning into My Mother

Childhood was boxes and crates and hope
chest and bunk bed and pillows and sleepless
nights and keep the light on for reading and
utility bills and cable bills and mortgage and
no insurance until 16 and scraped elbows and
chipped teeth and busted head from softball
and *it doesn't look like you need stitches* and
sewing patterns and newspapers and drawings
from preschool and expired Farmer Jack ads
and birth certificate somewhere around here
and holes in walls and no room to walk and
cigarette air and black-ring tub and is that a
roach and dog and catcatcat and hairy couch
and hairy chair and hairballs and dust balls and
moth balls and broken Bissell and five-foot
trophies and perfect attendance awards and
Lifetime originals and NCIS and *please record
The Nanny* and crusted pans and sticky pots
and food bank beans and mayonnaise
sandwiches and first kiss and first hand job
and first blow job and first bruise when
finds out and

man knees and man hands and man breath and
man beer and man vodka and man against man
and tantrums and bipolar and manic
depression and 9-1-1 and suicide attempts and
crying before school and growing up fast and
holding onto too much and

can't move and can't breathe and can't seem
to locate anything including an exit and
chances are I will lose sight of the mother and
perish inside this childhood.

Time Stands Still at My Local Kroger

The grocer, with his frozen produce hands, does not know
I am an orphan now.
The butcher was slicing
the Virginia Baked Ham
when the call came in.
I was on the phone for 30 seconds,
my grip still on the family
sized box of Life.
Time is deader than a five-day avocado,
deader than a razorback hog.

The butcher was slicing
ham thinner than the air in this building.
The stock boy's knees were bent
in an endless brown box serenity prayer.
Time is deader than a seven-day avocado,
deader than my intubated mother.
It feels like the cashier has been making change since February.

Hard Things

Today I get out of bed. Though I did not sleep. I shower. Undercook two eggs. And take the recycling to the curb.

Please hold your applause.

My short ride into the office is a blank. But it must have been successful. Because I am alive. And creating spreadsheets.

I read a kind email. Cry. Reread it. Cry again. I am not quite ready to believe in myself.

And then I work. A little. But mostly I wish I wasn't working.

There is an important meeting. I am not invited. But I vulture the leftover Qdoba placed in the lunchroom. That is when I notice, blessedly, that my appetite is back.

I make more spreadsheets.

On the way home from work, it is dark. And rainy. My astigmatism is reckless and at the wheel. Construction makes the freeway look like fucking spaghetti. I can't breathe. The asphalt swallows me with a long, black tongue.

Just kidding. But that's how life feels sometimes.

I make it home. I hang a painting. A commercially popular reprint that has been resting against my living room wall since before I stopped caring. It's crooked. But it's up.

For dinner, the grilled cheese I make is burnt at every angle. I eat it anyway. And feel sick. But not about the sandwich.

I wash my plate immediately. Scrub the frying pan. Leave them both to ~~die~~ dry.

And watch *Lost* until 10. When I put on my pajamas. And get into bed. Though I do not sleep.

Please clap.

The Second Is Fear

There are few things you have given me and not revoked. The first and most memorable: a barrel of monkeys. Orange barrel. Orange monkeys. Molded from the same sheet of plastic. Pawing at one another until the weight of family pulls them down.

Papa Bear

Last month Mom spent
$400 on the shirtless man
in her living room
She bought a steel box
as big as a brown bear
and said it was for Father's Day
She even asked for contributions
Whatever you can spare
Don't feel obligated

My obligation died
30 years ago
when his heart gave out

Fathers are like nipples
We all have them
Some are hairy
Some are useless
And some sit bare chested
in front of NASCAR races

An Influencer Follows Me on Twitter, and It Feels Like a Personal Achievement

My mom always told me when it's raining, tornadoes can't touch down. As if wind would fear water. Wind is the reason I fail. Like an airborne cow flailing in a virescent sky. But no air floods this vessel. I am lungless and spiraling. The responsibility of being something besides a steel skeleton coated in goldbeater's skin is too much. I'd rather be the sputtering balloon than the mighty dirigible. Maybe I'm terrified of shaping clouds into ambition. Maybe I am the condensation fearing the current. Look! Over there's a rabbit. See the long white ears?

Never mind, that's just the contrails of my tailspin.

February 17, 2021

If her legs are swollen and weeping water, pull the lowball down from the shelf. Run a clean towel inside the hollow and around the rim. If her oxygen level dips below 80, take the stainless-steel tongs and drop in two cubes of ice. If she is admitted to the ICU, pour a finger of rye whiskey. If she is intubated, pour two. If she contracts a staph infection in her lungs and E. coli in her urinary tract, even though the hospital is taking extra COVID precautions, pour one more. She is not coming home. If you make the call to pull the ventilator, add another finger and one more cube of ice to match the frigidness of this decision. If the hospital is restricting in-person visits but will allow you to peer through her window outside like she is a dying whale, slam the bottle because it is single degrees this February, and you will need the warmth.

Sibling Rivalry

He starts the conversation with *I don't always agree with the things you do.*

Followed by a long list of things he does not always agree with that I do.

Of course, I cannot get offended because my brother ends with *but I still love you because you're family.*

Twenty percent of meerkats are killed by their own kind.

If she senses a defect, a mother hamster will eat her tiny, pink pups.

Hyena cubs often attack siblings not yet emerged from the amniotic sac.

And once I called police with his hands gnawing at my throat.

When My Father Died
A golden shovel

Three years is too young to ask, *What's
wrong with Daddy?* His hair was brown
like graveside, eyes dark like closed casket. And
the Pepsi he held spilled brown and sticky
on the tile when it fell from his slack hand. A
final memory, something to stick.

I Killed My Mother

Rather, my medical power of attorney, a discouraging conversation with the doctor & an impossible decision killed my mother. Rather, COVID sanitation restrictions and infection from a ventilator killed my mother. Rather two bad lungs, one bad heart & 400 pounds killed my mother. Rather, 62 years of depression & bipolar killed my mother. Rather, two failed marriages, countless failed relationships & widowhood killed my mother. Rather, an alcoholic mother & a dead father killed my mother. Rather unfulfillment, unfettered loneliness & debilitation killed my mother. But isn't it easier to blame it on a daughter with her hand on the proverbial plug?

The First Year Without Her

I didn't want to dread today,

this anniversary,

or the memory of Mom in the hospital,

me in the snow drift.

So, I made the warmest thing I could think of:

scratch noodles, cut square, boiled in chicken stock.

They were probably too thick

but still reminded me of her.

And I ate a bowl while watching *Patsy & Loretta*,

a story about two women loving each other.

Even after death.

Fatality

Inseparable are the memories of my brother and me
playing Mortal Kombat on Nintendo 64
and him locking me out
of the house while a chuck roast browned in the oven.

He knew the buttons and the combos and the backstories.
I knew only the mustard yellow of Scorpion's tunic
and *back, back, A*.

As our mother pulled up in the drive,
her amethyst Plymouth Breeze barely at a stop,
he ran out squealing, *Lannie burnt the roast, Lannie burnt the roast!*

A claw bolts from a palm, over and over again,
until the power bar goes from bright to bloody to absent.
And he accused me of cheating.
Demanded a rematch.

But I was already inside, oven mitts on, tending to a dead thing.

It's the Year 2000, Cosmic Bowling Has Started, and I Think I'm Gay

I am Lannie's frozen skin // watching // the crisp //white back of a girl at the bowling alley // her graceful wrist attached to an 8-pound ball // The girl pulls back // extends // releases // ugly form // beautiful form // I am Lannie's gut sliding like oil down the lane // I am her dilating pupils //

I am Lannie's confused body // 13-years-old // daydreaming over cheap food stand nachos // Nipping at a corn chip with inexperienced lips // bright yellow cheese dripping // Watching the girl throw her head back // laugh //

I am Lannie's constricted throat // when asked *What the hell are you staring at?* // I am Lannie's pursed lips // holding back a retort sharper than shoulder blades // I am Lannie's crossed arms // wishing her stepfather wouldn't eye her // like a 7-10 split // Something // to be knocked down //

Dear Photo of My Dead Mother, Circa 1978

God, she looked happy. Look at those cheeks. Two doughy dinner rolls that she'll pass on to her daughter.

*

At our favorite Coney Island, I get a bowl of chicken lemon rice soup with a stale roll I never eat. Mom stuffs it in her purse. For later.

She orders a lamb gyro and a Pepsi with lemon.

*

She was 19 in the photo. I am told she was unhappy at 19. At 9. At 29…

*

Instead of draining the wedge into her soda, she peels the meat from the rind with her teeth. Her cheeks puckering with sour satisfaction.

*

There was a can of Pepsi on the coffee table. Perhaps the only habit she kept over the next 40 years. If you don't count depression.

Her lips were tight, an upturned line. A gutted slice of lemon.

*

But I see her in that booth, tearing into the lamb, and in my memory, I swear she is smiling.

Whiskers
A golden shovel

I wonder if his face would be smooth as the stones I
often pocketed to show him. Or if, even though I hated
it, he would run his rough cheek along mine, the facial
hair chafing. He possessed not a single crowning hair,
                                but
maybe he would grow a thick, dark ducktail to atone. It
seems irreverent, however, to hang a hat on how I grew
up without a whiskered, grinning jaw of a father. An on-
us thrust upon a sad stranger, a man who never knew me.

Oophagy (or Intrauterine Cannibalism)

Found poem: "Shark Cannibalism and Early Life" by Molly Edmonds

Shark pups depend on yolk.

The best-known cannibal
is the egg. Embryonic
teeth killing unborn
brothers and sisters

until one shark remains.

My Mother Deftly Misses the Point

I tell her *Billy stares at me*
Billy of the ponytail
of the chatter
of the unpaid rent
Billy the virtual stranger
whom I beg my mother
not to invite to Thanksgiving

He may have a lazy eye
she theorizes

Billy of the eyes I know are blue
and alert
because of how often I find them
across the room
and on my ass

I tell her I won't come to dinner
if Billy is there

She ignores the ultimatum and asks
Are you sure you don't mean Tim?

If Found

Lost: One suede varsity jacket, maroon, medium, purchased at Winkelman's on a day Mom let me skip school and go shopping with her. One Jersey Boys DVD, online purchase, intended Christmas present, we spent half the morning searching the house. Virginity, back when I felt so close to her, I thought this was a secret I couldn't keep. Weight, when she envied my size. Breath, every blue lip, every trip to the ICU left us also lungless and lost. One mother, winter, Time. Time. Time. Time. Time. Time.

Meet Me at the Funeral Home, I'll Be the One Cussing in the Foyer

Goddamn lock
in the goddamn pine
beneath the goddamn lining

Goddamn key
in the goddamn hands
of a goddamn mound of ash

Goddamn door
in the goddamn casket
leading to God knows where

Death

I dreamed I ran into him at a comic bookstore
in a state neither of us have ever been to.

I remember glancing out the show window
at a passing sedan, wondering if I had somehow

stumbled into downtown Chicago, where he lived,
300 miles away from me. We hugged. Tighter

than I've ever hugged a man I'd only learned
to trust on Twitter & over the phone that one time

last February. When my mom died, & I didn't know
how to cry in front of both a casket & a cheese platter.

When we pulled away, our arms thick with loss,
his smile melted into a stranger's teeth and hard jaw.

I said, *I'm sorry. I thought you were someone else,*
& he bashfully admitted, *Yeah, me too.*

The First Christmas Without Her

With desperate fingers, I pluck
the head out of its socket.
Which of course solves nothing.
Darkness remains in the tree.

*Why couldn't you last
just one more Christmas?*

This pre-lit frosted fir
was meant to make life easier

but a strand gave up
half-way down the cold, steel spine,
and I never had a parent

teach me about series circuits
and the patience to
check bulb by bulb by bulb.

Frankly, this grief is inconvenient.

A light goes out, and still,
I am expected to shine.

Words Between the Daughter and the Mother
After Lee Potts

1.
When thickening stew with flour,
the key to avoiding lumps
is to stir continuously
with a parent's absent hand.
Learn to read the surface
of a well-boiled white potato,
skinless and vulnerable.

2.
A child is taught to peel
and chop the carrots
with any edge she can find.
Sauté the yellow onions
with gentleness. Crush
the bouillon cubes.

3.
We are all meat
trying our damnedest
to be tender.

Self Portrait with Cremains

Google tells me cremation takes 4 to 15
business days. So, when the funeral home asks
me if I want to be present for the process,

I imagine a spare cot in the crematorium.
The pillow hard. The blanket thin.

I imagine breakfast, lunch, and dinner.
Blackened toast three times a day for three weeks.
Because pot roast just doesn't seem appropriate
when your mother is carbonizing.

I imagine a thick word search for company.
Circling terms like *aftercare, urn, columbarium, furnace*.

I imagine waking up in the middle of the night,
bladder full, the glow of the chamber
lighting my steps to the bathroom.

I imagine calling off work. *Sorry.*
I won't be in again today. They're pulverizing
the chunks of bone that didn't burn.

Rite of Passage

The first time I hit a man,
it was instinct. His hammy hands gripped my throat
like a butcher swinging at hindquarters.

There is still an ambivalence in my fist
when I think of it. A coalition of panic and dignity.
Because when my knuckles returned to me,
they wore a dress of red
from his cheek. A pelt from the recent kill.

"I Love You Like Baby Hitler Loved His Easy Bake Oven"

as a teen, i spent my days unraveling. hormones and limbs and identity. within months of nascent breasts, i discovered i could brand myself. could press a searing iron to the flesh of my own forearm. before anyone could tattoo it. i was the token. Jew.

not the religion or the nation. but the people, i insisted. hailing from my father's blood. which did not pitch me into the welcoming *brit bat* of judaism. but still friends interrogated me. about hanukkah, which i celebrated exactly once. an attempt to break bread with my dead father.

my mother was alive and well. and German. even without her absolute aryan features. i was a walking contradiction. a conflict of interest. i was willed to hate myself.

i grew adept at laughing through the cheap shots. at my supposed innate frugality. after all, i could discern a cent from a dime by the sound of its rattle. i became so skilled at self-deprecation. i would sling vicious jokes before anyone else could. even my expression of love was a grossly insensitive punchline. i guess that was the self-loathing.

because what kind of Jew lets her friends tell her she can ride in the ashtray. with all the other Holocaust victims? the dust of my ancestry. escaping at 90 mph on the freeway. as we all slammed our hands into the car roof with every blacked-out headlight.

The First Thanksgiving Without Her

We pick at this bird
with nimble fingers,
pull at the thick skin and meat
until there is nothing left.

And even when there is nothing,
we boil down its flightless spirit
for hot broth.

This bird came to our table
dead, and still
we find new ways to destroy it.

We lick our lips
at all the corpse has to give.

A Devotion, of Sorts

God, I have loved you since my mother's
plump lips praised you in the kitchen,
in the living room, in Aunt Joyce's
dining room during a hand of Gin Rummy.

My mother was devoted to you, God.
She even prayed to you during *SVU*.
And still, miraculously, she chose you
over Christopher Meloni.

She never needed whiskey, God.
Never needed that four pack
of Seagram's Escapes.
Not when Mom had you, a pen,
and a book full of word searches.

To be honest, God, when she drank of you
from her chipped H&R Block mug,
Mom often diluted your message
with cold water from the kitchen tap
because you are a strong and powerful god.

When I visited my mother as an adult,
sometimes, I would sit on her knees,
and, God, I would pray to you too.
From the same cup, from the same lips.

Now, you are all I have left of my mother.
She was formidable, and though I am not,
God, let me worship you from morning
until 3:00 pm, at the very latest.

Pantoum for Mom and Punxsutawney Phil

It's just the same day over and over and over and over and over, Mom says, explaining once again how much she hates the movie Groundhog Day. She does not see the benefit of reliving one day a thousand times or more and despises how a snowstorm can turn a selfish, arrogant prick into a god.

Every year, on February 2nd, Mom tells me she hates Groundhog Day, and every year, on February 2nd, I tell her how this movie changed my life. How God was a selfish, arrogant prick, and the snowstorm created a miracle. I tell Mom that Harold Ramis and Danny Rubin wrote the perfect parable.

Every year, on February 2nd, I let Groundhog Day change my life again. I feel the puddle, the cold shower, the toaster, the poetry, the song on repeat, and send a prayer to Bill Murray, thanking him for the perfect parable. But Mom has only her own experiences and doesn't understand that I am

the puddle, the cold shower, the toaster, the poetry, the song on repeat. She cannot recognize the miraculous sum of a thousand moving parts. Mom does not understand that I also experience her unwillingness to learn. She plays God, stirring up the same violent storms time and time again.

Mom refuses to accept that someday I will move away from her storm. She does not see the parable in reliving one day a thousand times or more, I watch Mom stir the same selfish, arrogant pricks time and time again, and it's the same day over and over and over and over and over and over and

You Ask Me How I Am but Never Wait for the Answer

Hello

It is our weekly phone call. Last week you wound me in stories of how well my brother is doing at his new job, slinging plastic around a pallet. A spider assembling meals. The waves of pride so violent they threatened the throat and lungs of your youngest sling. This week you tell me you're evicting him. But that trumpet's been blowing for twenty years. The notes are ants, shriveled and stuck to stale webs.

How are you?

Today I discovered I cannot rest with men. The severe insomnia in my twenties was from being fingered in my sleep on three separate occasions, proving there is no safety in numbers. But saying this would strop the lightning in your hands. I cannot afford to bold and underline the italics you bore me. Instead, I say *I'm fine.*

That's good

Sometimes, when you go on and on about my brother or your shingles or the dog, I sit in my car and watch leaves drip through birch branches. Like plucked and repudiated gray hairs. Like a damp robot. Like the water cycle of an evaporating family.

I love you

I don't doubt you love me. The same way I don't doubt the pressure of the ocean floor will also crush me.

Goodbye

Tears

I was five years old, you twelve.
You had a fit, as you did then.
Your face was a red onion: plump,
veiny, the skin straining purple

with rage. I remember our mother
weeping as if she had touched
your pungent temper then swiped
at the raw corners of her eyes.

You often affected us that way.
On the floor, your fists chopped at
the carpet like frenzied knives. I
grabbed the nearest object: a lamp-

shade, placed it on your steamed
head and you calmed down. Your
anger shedding its skin. My fear
of you growing one more layer.

She Is Unavailable for Lunch
A golden shovel

Breakfast with the old man, she says. Why
do these words prick like a Sunday morning fork? I don't

tell my friend her nonchalance eggs
on abandonment issues three decades strong. I don't tell

her the way she jokes
and name drops - like they'd

never experienced even the faintest hairline crack
- makes my blood boil. At each

lunch, she crows. I can't tell one dead parent from the other
absent parent, and I wish she'd just shut up.

The First Halloween Without Her

I was a clown
one year for Halloween.
I think I was seven, maybe eight.
Mom didn't sew much
but she stitched together scraps of
black, orange, teal, and maroon
—an unlikely family—
just because I asked her to.

This year, I am a ghost
from a Netflix series
that Mom never would've seen.
Because the last scary thing she watched
was her kids saying goodbye
on a palm-sized screen.

Explaining My Introversion to a Genocidist Sympathizer

My mother spoons strangers into the living room / like heaping mashed potatoes / She has been fasting all year / and her jaw is unsnapped / ready for gravy boats of colonizers / She places strange hands on the bird / says they've earned carving rights / just for invading our small country

My mother minces the cloves of her ears / stashes them in the breadcrumbs / with a dash of salt and pepper and blind eye / She will never understand / amid all this feast in my belly / I am starving

My mother awaits the fleet with armfuls of corn / golden and without nutrients / like currency / Every year she offers more / of herself / and they stalk our home / with bayonet eyes / and musket hands / Ever present / they grow in the fields now / god-like and vine-like / crawling all over my body / convinced they can convert our heathenry to a new world / in which we're swallowed

My mother does not sow grains of solitude / so her artful fingers cannot taste / the poison in the soil

The Most Dangerous Fish

When temper swims through a man's hands, he
    becomes a contaminated stream, growing scales thick
as convenience store bricks. When I was 12, the
    most dangerous fish was a bottle of cheap wallop. Two
bucks for 40 ounces of menace. We young minnows
    thrash our tails against the current, feeling for the dry
bank in our mothers' river. With gaping lips, we ask,
    Why must we remain belly up? And our mothers answer,
Because we are hooked on weakness. It's true
    what they say: The last thing a fish notices is water.

A Single Stitch

Every time I try
to knit together

today's sawtooth skin
& the wide wound of youth,

she is there to remind me
the laceration is but a scratch

I watch the lie puddle
under helpless knees

& cannot tell the medic
from the mother

Suicide Attempt, #Unknown

I, too, am just a teenager
doused in accelerant
running in front of a cop car
asking it to ignite me.

Piece by Piece in Lakeland

                I thought Florida was good to you.

You became a tall, bronze man
                                      I could not
                                        recognize.

        Six months of manual labor mutilated

the hulking body you once carried.
                                                  Oh,

that whittling southern sun.

                  But you returned, claiming

our cousin was not good to you.

I assumed he had only cut you down a size.
        When, years later, he was arrested

                                          for dismembering
                                          and disposing of a
                                          man,

                you said, *See? I told you*

                        he was taking me apart, piece by piece.

The Child Was Not Invited to the Funeral
A golden shovel

She spent the morning with elderly neighbors, while the
                                                        graveyard
shook with mourners. After all, a three-year-old looks
suspicious when grandma imagines tiny black pockets overcrowded
with aggies, then scattered onto the funeral home floor. People
                                                                 must-
ering courage to approach the casket, crashing headfirst be-
tween the pews instead. Imagine! Little girl watches her daddy dying
but cannot witness him boxed and commemorated to
                                                                       get
closure. At her age, she shouldn't even know the word *coffin*.

The First Fourth of July Without Her

My brother burned burgers
and filled a cooler with flavored water

that no one touched.
The lid kept falling off, clattering to the pavement,

startling us all a little every single time.
Anyway, it was easier to get a drink from the kitchen

if you were able to dodge the holes in the floor
and the crotch-sniffing German Shepherd.

But at least there was a place, for a moment,
that no one else was.

My niece's toddler wore a cranial helmet,
sat babbling in a play pen by himself.

I remember wishing for that kind of isolation and protection.
We spread Mom's ashes beneath a bush in the backyard.

My brother insisted it was her favorite spot,
something I don't recall her ever mentioning.

My older nephew was the first to say *I love you, GiGi.*
We all smiled, and those of us not crying yet, started.

The Feedback in a Conch Shell Is Both the Ocean and My Mother

I wouldn't call you pretty;
I'd call you plain, Mama Turtle said,
running a plump hand through hair
the color of unrefined wood.

She whispered, *smart, smart, smart*
into tendrils wrapped tightly
around her fingers.

The hatchling, stung, said nothing
except *thank you, Mama.*

And she grew up,
as hatchlings tend to do,

into a woman with half a shell.

When the ocean called her stupid,
she laughed
and corrected the grammar
of its waves.

When the ocean called her ugly,
she shrunk
into the pale sand,
praying for a fuller shell.

Every night, she dreams
of the tides reversing,

reaching back to whisper
new words to the perfect hatchling,
over and over again,

until she finally asks,

But, Mama, don't you know
I can be both?

Red Skies at Morn

What if conversations on compression socks are all we have now? What if my cloudburst eyes and inclement guilt are the only things I'm left with when I hang

up the phone? I'm scared there will only be the memory of a therapist's office, recalling the damp helplessness of growing up. Learning to pivot

from outpost to outrage. Realizing it was you I was angry with all along. On a clear day, you can see the bull shit.

With your legs weeping water, we both know you'll never see the ocean again. Why are we pretending there are windows to view rough skies? Only the hard mud

of memory remains, and already I have forgotten the pink of childhood. From here on out, there will only be talks of your health and the weather.

The Day My Mother Is Intubated, I Find a Pimple on My Chin

Her glasses are on the bedside table
when I walk in. If she were awake, I would be a blur,
but I still want to look my best.

What if this is the last time she sees me?

So, I tug the face mask lower,
hiding the blemish, but exposing
the top of my nose to the antiseptic room.

The nurse says the ventilator is at fifty percent
like it's a good thing, and doesn't mean
my mom has a 50/50 chance of leaving this room.

What do you wear when today could be
the last day your mother is alive?

A black sweater with screen-print hammerheads
because these past five years
have felt like a slow-motion shark attack.

Her eyes flutter, and I stuff one of the empty
miniature cokes in the sweater's long front pocket
as she has always taught me to do.

Ten cents, I hear her say.

When I look up, her eyes are open,
crinkling through the tubes and wires and pain,
and I forget about the goddamn pimple.

brother, brother, brother

when our father died // you became: the man of the house // steel beam in the basement // nine-year-old tantrum quaking beneath the ground floor // bo(d)y to walk over // something to frame //

but who said you could brick wall your shoulders like that? // who let you fortify those fists? // who made you the bunker you are today? //

when our father died // i became: the wraith in the mirror // summoned by three names // sugar bowl scraping across the kitchen table // cold spot near mom's favorite recliner // hollow tap-tapping each morning at precisely 2am // something to occupy the walls //

who says a young house can't feel haunted?

To the Lonely Spark

A boy
is sometimes
a utility.
With limbs

like spliced
cables.

Knotted

around
his Sega,
his favorite

anime,
and five
uninterrupted
minutes

with *Skinemax*
in his basement
bedroom.

He idolizes
Shawn Michaels
and X-Pac.

Loves how
they fight

off the ladies
with an arm
to the chest.

Boy throws

overlapped
wrists

onto his crotch
with gusto.

Suck it!

he snarls
at the tangled
sister
in the other
room.

Suck it!
He spits
at the man

in his father's
drunken skin.

Suck it!
he growls
at the eager
therapist

who says
*How are we
feeling today?*

and swears
she too
knows the
sensation

of frayed wires

and the short
fuse of a bipolar
body.

Suck it!
he whispers
to the lonely

spark.

A Widow Offering
A golden shovel

Not to sound skeptical / but I
am not sold / on this / heaven thing / Kids don't
need clouds in their throat / to trust
the dirt crowding / their fathers' mouths / Steps
1 and 2 are honesty / Step 3 is red herring / They
contradict / like the phrase / *shallow grave* / and are
clutched in little / beating fists / Nails always
digging / into peace / lily palms / up-
turned for God's next fish story / To
placate / A widow offering / something.

The First Birthday Without Her

My friend buys a home safe
and it sits in his living room
until he can find the perfect place for it.

I say, *My mom offered to get me a safe once—*
Nothing as big as yours.
Just enough room for documents
like birth certificates and the deed to the house.
She said it would be for my birthday.

But then she died.
I say it like a punchline,
barely holding back an elbow to his ribs
and a hissing *badoom ching.*

My friend's eyes are sad
when they look at me
and I know he's wondering
if I'm okay.
Or if maybe we need to pass a blunt
in the garage and talk
about how it's two years later
and I still can't sleep.

I say, *You're allowed to laugh.*
He does—because he's a good friend—
but it's soft and lost.

I laugh
harder than I probably should.

And I Will Carry This Burden

Into the ventilator,
my mother
mouths *I love you*,

collapses like a blue house
into the hospital gurney.

Our annual Easter gathering.

Three days later, extubated
& resurrected,
Mom asks how long
she would have lived if
she hadn't reached the ICU,
& the triage nurse,
after some persuasion,
estimates *maybe six hours.*

Still, Mom negotiates
with the dietician.
Whether Diet Pepsi
should replace regular,
if salad is *free.*

The attending nurse scoffs
when I mention Palliative
Care, as a precaution,
as a backup lung to survive
another Good Friday.
He jerks his head, shocked
at my suggestion,
& insists she is mulish
but healthy.

Crucified, I say to him,
Maybe I misunderstood.

Ode to 1997

I was a Junior Girl Scout
when my mother became Troop Leader.
It was the year she had us make
totem poles out of toilet paper rolls
for cultural enrichment,
and I wished she was cooler
because Sarah Lucas said
cardboard totem poles were lame.
It was the year Sarah Lucas
recited every line
from the live-action 101 Dalmatians
at Jamie Burroughs' sleepover,
even when all the girls begged her not to.
And Sarah Lucas
and I had to leave early
because the carpet irritated our skin.
It was the year Mom *was* cooler
and scheduled a mall lock-in.
While Claire's and the food court
drew in the other girls, Sarah Lucas
convinced me to do Karaoke.
We practiced Roy Orbison's Pretty Woman
until we knew the tempo
of every purr and every *mercy*
and every *wooooaaaooooh*.
But Sarah Lucas refused to sing,
leaving me on the stage alone.
It was the year Mom and I
went door-to-door hawking cookies.
We sold over 200 boxes,
far more than we ever had before,
but Sarah Lucas still sold the most.

Karen Kilgariff Says the Death of a Mother Is Like a Slow-motion Shark Attack

and the danger lurks

    within a tender body
        attended to by great white
            lab coats

                Consumption is
                a week-long special,
                      and everyone is tuning in

                        Panic ripples
                          through the daughter
                            like an endless wave
                            of teeth

                                Mama drops

                                      from her mouth,
                                      one more fossil
                                      on the ocean
                                      floor

Where to Start

Found poem: Eragon by Christopher Paolini, prologue

       In this story,
the boy
       does not stay
a boy
       He becomes thick
       like plot,
       angry
       like antagonist

The non-boy
       leaves
       his sister
       to the monsters

       It is
the ~~boy's~~
       story

       She is barely in it

Happy Mask Shop

After Zelda: Ocarina of Time

Listen, in here,
we are all green boys
with wooden shields,
saying good-bye
to the trees
who die to protect us

We forsake the map
& compass
& fairy
that point us
toward the castle

We ignore the owl

Hey, out there,
the pots are fragile,
cash grows wild
& the gilded spider
is a metaphor

We know the sun's song,
can even grip the hilt
of the morning,
& one day
we will leave
this childish skin behind

My Father Wears a Hawaiian Shirt to Die In

I don't remember him
besides hide and seek,
a perfect pair
of slippers calling out
as I titter beneath a crib.
But everyone weathered with
my blood says I was daddy's girl.
I helped him fold and tuck.
A bed, laundry, the lining of
his casket.
He was patient
as the earth.
A Baptist minister, he never
swore. Two things orbited him:
Jewish ancestry. A dark and obvious comet
he feared
might plummet on Germanic command.
And a dim horseshoe of hair. Like
nailing it between his ears
would bring him
luck. But still
he died
at the kitchen table,
in a Hawaiian shirt,
with a Pepsi in his hand.
A last word
like gas through his teeth:
Shit.

The First Easter Without Her

I am reminded of ham.

And my mother in the ICU—
not the last time, but the time before that—
her red legs rupturing from CHF.
Her doctor limiting both sodium and water,
warning, *Now, Debbie,*
I don't want to see you back in here.

I am reminded of a phone call a week later
Mom, how's the diet going?

Her telling me the fridge went out again,
and the only way to save the capicola
was to eat sandwiches every day,
washed down with slices of watermelon.

I am reminded she lived
less than a year after that conversation.

I Tell Myself She Ran Away

My couch cushions furried within hours
of the last departed guest.

The mantle clock, stopped at 5:10
three evenings prior, was lightly coated,

and I could think only how thankful I was
the baked ziti had not been ruined.

Within a week, the floor disappeared,
succumbing to a deluge of dander.

I began buying lint brushes in bulk,
hired a cleaning crew, vacuum salesmen

knew me by name. I tried everything
to make it right again. To feel alive,

I slammed every door, but they closed
gently and infuriatingly against the hair.

The lamps, muted by a thick ginger dust,
plunged me into further darkness.

Once the big picture window was covered,
the neighbors stopped calling.

When I could no longer see the television,
I just decided to sleep.

Blankets of fur provided soft, extra layers
to the ruckled bed, and honestly,

I kinda liked that part. Sometimes,

sometimes, I could rest through the night

without the nightmares in which
I suffocated under the weight of it all.

At some point, the cat was lost. I could
not discern her from the invasive piles.

I tell myself she ran away. An offense
more sufferable than the alternative.

I Won't Be Able to Make It to the Cemetery Today; I'm Lowkey Annoyed
After tweet by @Lefty_TaughtYOU

The bodies in black wool remind me of my own skin
—how I couldn't bag it and give it away

Mom always told me I look maudlin in dark shades
The sun could split the pines behind the mausoleum,

teeter the doleful gravestones like dominoes,
and plow through my buried heart. Still, she would say,

hydrogen has always been her color.

I Just Emailed an Estate Lawyer Regarding My Mother's Will Using the Subject Line "I Really Don't Know What to Title This"

Subject: ~~Deceased Mother~~
~~Probate for Deceased Mother~~
~~I Need a Probate Lawyer~~
~~Help, My Mother Is Dead~~

I am ~~the estranged and grieving daughter~~ writing on behalf of my ~~manic-depressive~~ mother, who ~~spent 62 years slowly piecing herself out~~ died this past Wednesday evening, ~~alone~~. She named me executor of her will, and I'm hoping you and I can discuss rates, process, and ~~my abandonment of her~~ expectations. To be honest, I am at a loss on how to proceed with ~~all this guilt~~ the things she left behind: ~~Great-grandchildren, a son, and a daughter who will never again see the crinkle of kind, misguided blue eyes~~. I understand her assets may be placed in probate to ~~feed the~~ satisfy creditors. After all, my mother had a lot of ~~heart~~ debt.

As I am currently on ~~overdrive to ignore the pain~~ bereavement for the next five days, meeting this week would be ~~excruciating~~ preferable. Please reply with your availability, and I will ~~shower, brush my hair, and force myself~~ do my best to meet it.

I appreciate any and all help you can provide during this difficult and confusing ~~torture~~ time.

On Pennsylvania Road

We played Barbies vs G.I. Joes // You were Ken // and you let me be Snake Eyes // When my first crush was your friend Donny // *sitting in a tree* spilled from your mouth like branches in the soil // I think you liked the idea of me wanting something of yours // Once, I theorized our mother was dead // because it was snowing // and her car had yet to pull in the drive // I couldn't stop crying // but you insisted it wasn't true // and she was just around the corner // The day the walls caught on fire // you let me show you what I learned when Ronald McDonald visited school // And we crawled on our bellies to safety // Even when - in one of your fits - you lurched like a bear taking down the campsite // I was the only one who could calm you // Armed with a lampshade to dim your mania // Do you remember this closeness? // Brother and sister taking on a broken home // Before you became the broken // Before I shunned the home //

Pot Roast, Unburnt

Let's go back in time; rewind
      to the lost boy in the woods.

      To the frailty of shared molecules
and the aggressive scent of burning

pot roast whose only thought
      was to tenderize for family.

      As unsullied siblings, let us return
to when we didn't catch dirty jokes

in Saturday morning cartoons.
      Or you did but still let me laugh

      along, fresh and impressionable. I
don't know when regard became

rivalry became panic became
      rabbit became snake became pit

      but I know I trusted you once
or twice. Maybe it was puberty,

fury growing faster than our cells.
      Or our fervent disagreement on

      button smashing. Or maybe fire
was the only role model we had.

My Worship
A golden shovel

If you had not collapsed at the kitchen table that day, I can't tell you how
often I'd beg to make the bed with you, tucking Navy corners. The many
times I'd squeal—equal parts preparation and reckless giggle—for tickles,
like the catfish in that YouTube video. Hands up, tummy exposed, does
it get any better than that? If my worship was a dive light, it
would blind the great barracuda. If it was a dead parent, its ghost would take
up residence in the elbow of the kitchen sink. My worship knows how to
sail on imagination and brace for oncoming waves of a make-
believe future. If my worship was weighed it would be heavier than
a harbor tugboat. If my worship grew limbs, it would be an octopus
squeezing me the way I've needed. And we would laugh laugh laugh laugh
until Mom looked at us like two unhinged Argonauts with a ten-
dacy to get too loud in the backyard pool, losing ourselves in a sea of tickles.

The First Month Without Her

No one prepares you
for how often you will say "my mother died"
to well-mannered strangers

> to close an account
> to distract yourself
> to erase a debt

How they will say "I'm sorry for your loss,"
and you will say "Thank you"
for this polite and hollow gift

The Only Thing I Wanted Was for You to Live

long enough
to meet your granddaughter.
Her pumping fists
narrowly avoiding a butterfly
closure in your arm.
The ventilator hissing.
Blowing kisses
with purple fingers
& white lips encumbered
by an endotracheal tube.
Still smiling, always smiling.
Hoping we, &
this fabricated memory,
will somehow endure.

The Birch Is Too Proud

When I've crashed
through the thicket
nose first,   truths
plucked like berries,
fists grown into thorns.
I am too sapling,
too snapped.
Axes like shadows.

When I've gnashed bread
crumbs between tired teeth.
My own lost fingers picked
carefully from the path.
Knowing this forest
will never return to me,
and I will never   return
to the forest.

When I've beaten these
branches to splinters, bark
flicking off knotted
knuckles that know only
how to push up
and away from a trunk
ringed by years
of cornflower eyes going   dark.

Will
      you
           be
                  proud
                       then?

I Imagine My Mother Apologizing

I didn't keep you
safe, and you deserved more
than the sharks
I let past the threshold.
I gargled malt liquor
men, let their brokenness
clink in the back of my throat.
Like ice in a sink,
reducing their guns to chum.
It never mattered
that their fists tore through
your childhood,
forcing you to emerge
as undertow. Every time
I let them spread
their palms over your thighs,
your fine baby sand turned to glass
-weapons for a flood
you never should have
breast stroked in
I was self-involved and
self-indulgent and
selfishselfishselfish.
I hope you can forgive me.

My Brother Puts Me in a Boston Crab Underwater, and I Stop Breathing

When you're drowning,
everything is the speed of a man
a p o l o g i z i n g .

Rough Draft
After Malcom Friend's "Cover: 'I Just Can't Stop Loving You'"

Dear Eric,

I can forgive, but I can't forget.

~~Dear Eric,~~

~~When mom had a seizure in the dining room,~~

~~it was like an opening scene from C.S.I.~~

~~She'd broken her nose on the edge of the table,~~

~~gushing blood all over the original hardwood floors.~~

~~Do you remember how you panicked, stood there~~

~~screaming *Mom! Mom! Mom!* until I told you to call 9-1-1?~~

~~I requested a pillow for her head, and turned her,~~

~~to keep her tongue from juddering down her throat.~~

~~I asked what time it was, had you write it down.~~

~~When the paramedics arrived, they lauded us,~~

~~claimed we may have saved her life.~~

~~When I say I can forgive you, but I can't forget~~

~~what we went through together, please know~~

~~it means this moment too.~~

After Further Consideration, She Has His Ears
A golden shovel

What
     memory do
     you bequeath a daughter who will not remember you?
What does she call
     you, if not *someone*
     from a thirty-year-old longing? You leave her with
an endonym but no
     identity. Your body
     not dead enough, your lore not feather enough, and
she will grow up with no-
     thing. Even her nose
     is her mother's. She will ask about you. But nobody
knows.

Birding

You were everyone's mama robin, cracking
a warm egg over the fledglings in the neighborhood.

I could not move without brushing against the wings
of your adopted flock,

even as I squawked for the nest to empty.

After all, shouldn't blood paint your red breast
without the stretch of hungry necks?

This maternal clutching, this
communal roosting, is how I found myself

sniped and unfeathered,

watching mama robin cooing and mama robin chirring
and mama robin loving all the birds.

Death Leaves Something Behind

I did not spend much time wondering why his coat was at your house, only that it was dark and dripping from the fur-covered rocking chair.

I picked it up to brush it clean, batted the sleeves with shaky hands, stirred the surplus of cat hair into the smoky air of your living room.

The wool irritated my skin, but I slipped the coat on anyway.
A form of masochism I have never quite shed from childhood.

My nose wrinkled from the sweet scent of White Diamonds wafting from the fabric, and I was thankful the weight nor perfume fit me.

But when I tucked my fists into its silk-lined pockets, I found crumpled tissues, as my own pockets often contained. A sign

that perhaps he was more considerate than I had originally thought, and perhaps you had no choice but to invite him in for a last coffee.

I did not spend much time wondering why you let him into your house, I only wondered how long before his knuckles rapped at my door.

Now. Then. Always.

A golden shovel

"Listen, was I born gay, or did Julia Stiles in '10 Things I Hate About You' make me gay? It's literally impossible to know."
— Kate Stayman-London, <u>One to Watch</u>

My mom is watching Pretty Woman, and I am listen-
ing behind the couch. Sorry. That's not right. My mom *was*
watching Pretty Woman, and I *wasn't* being watched. I
try to remember that neglected girl is gone. Born
and elongated into a mess of a woman with short, gay
limbs that couldn't fit around a body if a body let her try. Or
I wish I had played with matches and nylons, but I never did.
Around the arm of the couch, a dirty child watched Julia
Roberts run her hands down a boot. One of the hostiles
now, I am a pair of pantyhose with a run. Snagged in
mid-air. Ogling both Vivian *and* Edward. At 10-
years-old, a woman's shoulder blades were things
I tucked under the cool covers of a twin bed at night, and I
would think about my stepfather who might hate
me if he knew. Might hit me if he knew about
the penis I touched in his pop-up camper. All you
ask for, as a child, is welfare. For a parent to make
a little noise when you're around. But maybe that's just me,
needing to be safe and whole and free and wanted. A nosegay
in the weeds, plucked by a kind hand that knits
daily flower crowns for her daughter, her prize. I literally
cannot think of a better ending than my mother's impossible
hands holding me now, then, always. Clinging to
to a future she didn't understand and a past I couldn't know.

Cremation: Mother

A casket burning
does not ask, *why is it so hot in this room?*
It is there for one thing only:

to hug a body
until there is no body left to hug.

Arguing the Etymology of "OK" with Someone Who's Always Been Fine

I tell her it started when I was six years old: the fear of spark, the fear of smoke, the fear of burning down with the house. I am: the walls containing a kitchen fire, soup on the stove, Mom forgetting to turn off the burner. The hambone crisping. The navy beans shriveling. A girl, crawling on an empty belly, pressing her hand against every door, searching for safety. Waiting to be engulfed.

She says I've experienced trauma. That my amygdala still thinks I am six and trapped and inhaling darkness.

I tell her Ronald McDonald came to my elementary school and taught me how to fight fires. And by *fight*, I mean run away. When I told my mother Ronald singed a bible just to show how flammable everything truly can be, she did not believe me. My mother never believed me where men were concerned.

She says I must be misremembering the part about the bible.

I tell her I have never been safe. Before the house fire. Before my amygdala developed. Before Carl and James and Chris and Brian and Benny and Michael and David and Paul and Ron and Abdul and Merle and Andrew and Timmy and Billy and all the other men who scorched everything I've ever held faith in. How can I be when even this conversation is tinder?

She says we've made good progress and she will see me next week.

I tell her her clothes smell like smoke.

The First Day Without Her

This morning, my mother's dead hand is emerging
from my cup of black coffee, dripping
like a lonely river birch.
Her nails are thick and uncut, fingers
strong, as I remember them.
At first, as her arm extends, I am unsure
what she is searching for.
The bowl of sugar? A spoon? My throat?
I clasp my fingers around hers,
touching her for the first time since the last time,
and we are still.

Acknowledgments

Thank you to these publications, in which the following pieces originally appeared:

Cephalopress: Inksac, "Now. Then. Always."

Emerge Journal, "I Killed My Mother," "brother, brother, brother"

Entropy, "Birding"

FERAL: A Journal of Poetry and Art, "You Ask Me How I Am but Never Wait for the Answer"

From Whispers to Roars, "Karen Kilgariff Says the Death of a Mother Is Like a Slow-motion Shark Attack"

Frontier Poetry, "On Pennsylvania Road"

ISACOUSTIC, "Explaining My Introversion to a Genocidist Sympathizer"

Kissing Dynamite Poetry Press, "Whiskers," "She Is Unavailable for Lunch," "When My Father Died," "In Tandem"

Lavender Bones, "The Time My Brother Doused Himself in Gasoline and Struck a Match Has Stolen the Remote"

Life in Quarantine—Stanford Project, "A Widow Offering," "After Further Consideration, She Has His Ears," "My Worship," "The Child Was Not Invited to the Funeral," "The Grand Canyon Is My Father"

Marias at Sampaguitas, "Papa Bear" (June 10, 2019 Weekly Contest Winner), "A Parable of Wanderlust" (Best of the Net 2019 nominee)

MORIA, "Sibling Rivalry," "Pot Roast, Unburnt"

Neon Hemlock Press, "A Single Stitch," "I Imagine My Mother Apologizing," "I Love You Like Baby Hitler Loved His Easy Bake Oven," "My Birth Has Often Been About Secrets," "The Birch Is Too Proud," "Rite of Passage"

Parentheses Journal, "The Most Dangerous Fish"

Pidgeonholes, "My Father Wears a Hawaiian Shirt to Die In" (THE BODY Contest semi-finalist)

Random Sample Review, "Pantoum for Mom and Punxsutawney Phil"

Selcouth Station, "Red Skies at Morn," "I won't be able to make it to the cemetery today; I'm lowkey annoyed," "My Brother Was a Bomb"

Southchild Lit, "To the Lonely Spark"

Stentorian Bitch, "Piece by Piece in Lakeland"

Stick Figure Poetry, "Time Stands Still at My Local Kroger"

Stone Circle Review, "If You Want to Be a Good Day"

TERSE. Journal, "The Wall"

The Coop: A Poetry Cooperative, "Arguing the Etymology of 'OK' with Someone Who's Always Been Fine," "Self-Portrait with Cremains," "I Just Emailed an Estate Lawyer Regarding My Mother's Will Using the Subject Line 'I Really Don't Know What to Title This'"

The Daily Drunk – Mall Rats Anthology, "Ode to 1997"

The Hellebore, "A Standing Dinner Invitation to My Anger"

The Red Lemon Review, "It's the Year 2000, Cosmic Bowling Has Started, and I Think I'm Gay"

The TEMZ Review, "My Greatest Fear Is Turning into My Mother"

Two Fingers Lit, "Fatality," "Rough Draft"

Author's Notes

Thank you to my family: my mother; my father; my brother; Kaitlyn, my wife; Dawson, our daughter. These poems would not exist without you.

Thank you to my friends. Especially Max, who has bought every book I've ever written and attended more events than I can even count.

Thank you to Hannah Grieco, Dr. Taylor Byas, and Todd Dillard, who have said such kind things about this book but have also shown so much support behind the scenes for years.

Finally, thank you to my editor, Beth Gordon. When you came to woo me on behalf of Animal Heart Press, little did you know, I was sold as soon as I knew I would get to work with you. But it's still nice to be wooed.

About the Author

Lannie Stabile (she/her), a queer Detroiter, is the winner of OutWrite's 2020 Chapbook Competition in Poetry and a back-to-back semifinalist for the Button Poetry Chapbook Contest. Lannie was also named a 2020 Best of the Net finalist. Her debut poetry full-length, *Good Morning to Everyone Except Men Who Name Their Dogs Zeus*, was published in 2021 by Cephalopress. Her fiction debut, *Something Dead in Everything*, is out now with ELJ Editions. Find her on Twitter @LannieStabile or lanniestabile.com.

www.ingramcontent.com/pod-product-compliance
Lightning Source LLC
Chambersburg PA
CBHW060033180426
43196CB00045B/2647